PREHISTORIC SAF

KILLER DINOSAURS

Liz Miles

RiverStream

Hardcover edition first published in 2012 by Arcturus Publishing

Hardcover Library bound edition distributed by Black Rabbit Books
P. O. Box 3263
Mankato
Minnesota MN 56002

Published by arrangement with Arcturus Publishing

Printed in China

Library of Congress Cataloging-in-Publication Data

Miles, Liz.
  Killer dinosaurs / by Liz Miles.
      p. cm. – (Prehistoric safari)
  Includes index.
  ISBN 978-1-84858-569-0 (hardcover, library bound)
  1. Dinosaurs–Juvenile literature. I. Title.
  QE861.5.M5537 2013
  567.9–dc23

                            2011051449

Text: Liz Miles
Editor: Joe Harris
Picture researcher: Joe Harris
Design: Emma Randall
Cover design: Emma Randall

Picture credits:
De Agostini Picture Library: 7tr, 7br, 13br, 15cr, 9tr, 19cr, 19br, 29tr, 29br. Highlights
for Children, Inc: 15tr. Miles Kelly Publishing Ltd: 11cr, 11br, 15br, 17br, 21tr. National
Geographic: 2–3, 24–25, 25tr, 25cr. Natural History Museum, London: 7cr, 13tr, 21cr.
pixel-shack.com: cover (main), 1, 5br, 8–9, 10–11, 11tr, 12–13, 14–15, 16–17, 17cr,
18–19, 20–21, 22–23, 23tr, 26–27, 28t, 29tc. Shutterstock: cover (all images top row),
4–5, 5tr, 5cr, 6–7, 9cr, 9br, 17tr, 23br, 27tr, 27cr, 27br, 29 (all except tc, tr, br).
Wikimedia: 13cr, 21br, 23cr, 25br.

SL002123US

1 2 3 4 5 CG 15 14 13 12
RiverStream Publishing—Corporate Graphics, Mankato, MN—122012—1008CGF12
Paperback version printed in the USA

CONTENTS

KILLER SAFARI

Are you ready for the adventure of a lifetime? You're about to set off on a journey across a mysterious island where killer dinosaurs live. Your mission is to film the most terrifying monsters of the prehistoric past. You will come face-to-face with hungry meat-eaters. This safari is going to be incredibly risky!

Before you set out, you check that you have all your supplies. To cope with the tricky island terrain—and to make quick escapes from deadly dinosaurs—you have brought an ATV (all terrain vehicle).

Soon you will be meeting killer dinosaurs like *Tyrannosaurus rex*—its head is nearly as long as you are tall. Beware those giant teeth. They could crush you like a bug!

SAFARI ESSENTIALS

Bones You are unlikely to need bones for bait—hungry dinosaurs will smell you out. However, a tasty bone might distract a charging killer long enough for you to escape.

Video camera As well as still shots of dinosaurs, video recordings are essential for capturing them in battle.

Your boat anchors offshore. You nervously drive your ATV down a ramp, through shallow waters, and across a rocky shore. You gasp at the sight of howling *Apatosaurus* as you speed over a grassy hill.

dinoPad All the dinosaur facts you need have been downloaded onto your electronic reader. You'll know which dinosaurs to fear the most.

SMALL BUT DEADLY

Just five minutes into your safari, you are reminded that killers come in all sizes. A herd of *Compsognathus* runs past, their bodies little bigger than chickens. You see one snap up a lizard, then run off, chewing noisily. You have barely set up your camera when something bigger suddenly looms into shot...

It stretches its flexible, long neck to catch prey between its small, sharp teeth.

The long tail helps it keep its balance as it runs.

The grasping fingers are useful for keeping a tight hold on a lizard or small mammal, ready for the first tasty bite.

Compsognathus is one of the smallest dinosaurs ever found.

Meaning of name: Pretty jaw
Height: 2 ft, 4 in (0.7 m)
Length: 4 ft, 7 in (1.4 m)
Family: Compsognathidae
Period: Late Cretaceous
Weight: 6.6 lb (3 kg)
Found in: France, Germany
Diet: Meat

The carnivorous (meat-eating) *Compsognathus* spends most of its time looking for small creatures to eat.

LITTLE MEAT-EATERS

Small killer dinosaurs use many different deadly hunting techniques.

▼ *Sinornithosaurus* may have grooved fangs, similar to a snake's.

▼ *Avimimus* is fast-moving and has a large brain for the size of its body, which suggests that it is capable of planning speedy surprise attacks.

▼ *Syntarsus* attacks in packs. By hunting in groups, it can bring down larger prey.

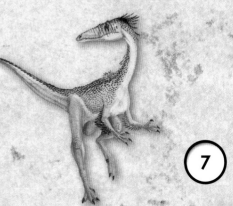

FLESH-EATING BULL

You find yourself face-to-face with a huge dinosaur—the horned *Carnotaurus*. It sniffs the air and then, as if it's caught a whiff of its prey or a competitor, it roars. Twisting its head, it glares at you. Perhaps your clothes hide the smell of your flesh because it pounds past, tracking the scent of something else. You follow from a safe distance in the ATV.

Carnotaurus' small horns are useful in a head-butting battle with a competing theropod or a fight with a rival over a mate.

It has sharp meat-tearing teeth but unusually weak jaws for a creature that needs to bite through skin and bone.

Carnotaurus is a meat-eater with an unusually weak jaw.

Meaning of name: Meat-eating bull
Height: 9 ft, 10 in (3 m)
Length: 25 ft (7.5 m)
Family: Abelisauridae
Period: Late Cretaceous
Weight: 1.1 tons (1,000 kg)
Found in: Argentina
Diet: Meat

The skin is a mass of pebble-like scales, becoming larger toward the spine. Skin impressions of nearly the entire body have given scientists an unusually clear idea of its bumpy skin.

TRACKING WITH THE SENSES

◄ The skull of the *Carnotaurus* shows it probably has an acute sense of smell—useful for tracking down its next live meal.

► Killer dinosaurs like *Carnotaurus* and *Tyrannosaurus* have simple ears—holes through which sound vibrations pass down nerve canals to the brain.

▼ *Carnotaurus*, like other theropod dinosaurs, has forward-facing eyes. These give it binocular vision, which helps it to judge the distance of its prey.

These stumpy arms are the shortest of any meat-eater.

HEAVYWEIGHTS

As you round an outcrop you come upon the *Carnotaurus'* prey: a spiky stegosaur. But another carnivore—an *Allosaurus*—is already on the scene. The *Allosaurus* tears at the plant-eater's vulnerable underbelly with its bladelike teeth. The stegosaur lashes out with its tail, but soon stumbles to the ground with exhaustion. You watch as the carnivores fight over its body.

A hungry *Allosaurus* won't be put off by the protective spikes of a stegosaur. However, it would prefer a sick or dead dinosaur that can't put up a fight.

Expandable cheeks mean that *Allosaurus* can bite off big chunks of meat to swallow whole.

Sharp serrated teeth, some twice the length of your finger, can cut through skin and flesh like a saw.

Allosaurus was at the top of the food chain in Jurassic times, and was the biggest carnivore on the planet for 10 million years.

Meaning of name: Different lizard
Height: 16 ft, 6 in (5 m)
Length: 40 ft (12 m)
Family: Allosauridae
Period: Late Jurassic
Weight: 1.5 tons (1,400 kg)
Found in: North America, Australia, Tanzania
Diet: Meat

The *Huayanosaurus* is a stegosaur with an impressive array of plates and spikes.

SLOW COACHES
How fast can these big, heavy killers move?

▶ *Allosaurus* carries its huge weight on two feet. Fossils show that it often falls when running fast, so sprinting is probably used as a last option.

▼ Stegosaurs move at about 4.3 mph (7 km/h), while a short-armed theropod like the *Allosaurus* manages at least 20 mph (32 km/h).

▶ A giant sauropod like an *Apatosaurus* moves only as fast as a person walking. So to catch an *Apatosaurus*, the *Allosaurus* won't have to rush.

NIGHT HUNTERS

As night falls you set up infrared lights and wait silently to see what you can catch on film. Suddenly there's a roar, and sounds of a scuffle. A pack of *Troodon* surround a *Triceratops*! The *Troodon* pounce with their tearing, sickle-shaped claws, and serrated teeth—but the *Triceratops* puts up a tough fight. Soon the pack gives up, leaving to find easier game.

The plant-eating *Triceratops* relies on its sharp, 3 ft- (1 m-) long horns to scare off the attackers.

Troodon is seen as the brightest dinosaur, with the biggest brain in proportion to its body weight.

Large, forward-facing eyes mean *Troodon* can judge distances easily. It seems to have good nocturnal vision.

SEEING IN THE DARK

▶ Big eyes suggest good nocturnal vision. The 1.5 ft- (0.5 m-) high *Dromaeosaurus* has huge eyes for the size of its body.

▼ Scientists measure rings of bone in the fossils of dinosaur eyes to estimate how well they could see in the dark. *Velociraptors* were probably among the dinosaurs that hunted at night.

▲ Eye fossil evidence suggests herbivores, such as *Diplodocus*, might have grazed at night too. To keep their vast bodies alive, long grazing hours may have been necessary.

TERRIFYING TYRANT

Your early morning alarm is a blood-curdling roar. You grab your camera, start up the ATV, and race toward the sound. It's the biggest dino movie star of them all: *Tyrannosaurus rex*. The monster's strong jaws pick up and shake its victim, an *Iguanodon*. The "tyrant lizard" uses its fanglike teeth to rip through the skin.

Tyrannosaurus teeth can crush bone. They can be up to 6 in (15 cm) long.

Stretch your arms wide and the length from fingertip to fingertip is about the length of the *Tyrannosaurus* jaw—4.6 ft (1.4 m).

Tyrannosaurus rex is the best known of all the dinosaurs.

Meaning of name: Tyrant lizard king
Height: 19 ft, 7 in (6 m)
Length: 46 ft (14 m)
Family: Tyrannosaur
Period: Late Cretaceous
Weight: 7.7 tons (7,000 kg)
Found in: North America
Diet: Meat

Tyrannosaurus' arms are too short to reach their mouths. However, they can be used for clutching prey or for steadying themselves as they stand up.

KILLERS' TEETH

▶ *Giganotosaurus*' teeth are smaller and narrower than the *Tyrannosaurus*' bone-crushers. However, they are better for slicing into the flesh of its prey.

▶ *Acrocanthosaurus* has 68 long, knifelike teeth. Like many theropods' teeth, they are curved and serrated. They are constantly shed and replaced by new teeth that grow in rows.

▶ *Dilophosaurus* has the teeth of a scavenger rather than a killer. The weak jaw and sharp teeth are better for plucking meat from a corpse and lack the strength to stab or grab a living dinosaur.

BATTLE TAILS

Another monster lumbers into view—an *Ankylosaurus*. The *T. rex* seems confused by the sudden appearance of this new opponent. As the predator hesitates, the *Ankylosaurus* swings its muscular tail toward its head. You duck as it whizzes past!

A two-legged predator like *T. rex* is especially vulnerable to *Ankylosaurus'* deadly club.

Ankylosaurus' back and sides are covered with thick armor. The *T. rex* aims to toss it onto its back.

Ankylosaurus is one of the most heavily armored dinosaurs ever found.

Meaning of name: Stiff lizard
Height: 4 ft (1.2 m)
Length: 23 ft (7 m)
Family: Ankylosauridae
Period: Late Cretaceous
Weight: 4.4 tons (4,000 kg)
Found in: Canada, USA
Diet: Plants

The knob at the end of the *Ankylosaurus'* tail is made up of bony plates fused together.

The "handle" of the club is made up of tendons that have partly turned to bone (ossified).

WEAPON TAILS: CLUBS, WHIPS, AND SPIKES

▶ **Tail clubs** Members of the ankylosaurid family, such as *Ankylosaurus*, are the best-known users of tail clubs. However, they are also used by dinosaurs such as the long-necked *Shunosaurus*.

◀ **Whip tails** *Brachiosaurus* flick out their long tails in a whiplike motion, knocking down predators. This gives them the opportunity to trample on their enemies while they are off-balance.

▶ **Tail spikes** Some plant-eaters, such as *Stegosaurus*, have tails ending with spikes. When threatened, a *Stegosaurus* will plant its back legs squarely, and use its front legs to swing its whole body, giving extra momentum to its tail.

FEET FIGHTERS

The epic battle ends in stalemate, and the *Tyrannosaurus* and *Ankylosaurus* leave, blood pouring from cuts and bites. As you walk back to the ATV, a group of fast-moving predators bursts through the bushes. These sleek raptors—called *Deinonychus*—are about your height, and they move fast. You only just make it to your ATV in one piece!

To bring down a smaller target, a raptor stabs a sickle claw into its victim, then drags it in a backward or downward motion across its flesh.

Deinonychus' sickle claws are so large they have to be raised when the dinosaur runs.

Deinonychus is far from the biggest dinosaur on the planet, but its intelligence, agility, and group hunting tactics made it one of the most fearsome.

Meaning of name: Terrible claw
Height: 5 ft (1.5 m)
Length: 10 ft (3 m)
Family: Dromaeosauridae
Period: Late Cretaceous
Weight: 180 lb (80 kg)
Found in: USA
Diet: Meat

CRUEL CLAWS

▼ The second toe on the *Deinonychus'* hind foot is unusually large—about 5 in (12 cm) long—and shaped like a sickle.

▼ **Velociraptor** is the most famous raptor. However, it is often misrepresented as being as tall as *Deinonychus*; in fact it is only about 3 ft (1 m) tall.

When a pack of *Deinonychus* jumps on a large victim, they use their hook claws like crampons. As they climb upward, they tear at vulnerable spots with their sharp teeth.

◄ **Troodon** is notable not just for its sickle claws, but also for its teeth, which have serrated sides like a saw.

SCAVENGING SWARM

Time to play it safe for a while. You drive the ATV up a sandy slope, and build a blind from branches. After a while, a swarm of *Coelophysis* rushes down the slope. Their tails sweep side-to-side like rudders. You follow, and see that they have discovered a carcass. Your camera records how they share their prey; some act as lookouts, while others take turns to eat.

These slim hunters with long tails and long necks are built to run fast. Like birds, they have hollow bones to keep them lightweight.

Coelophysis are not only hunters but probably scavengers too. Fossil contents of a *Coelophysis* stomach suggest that they could even be cannibals.

Coelophysis are known to gather together in packs. They may do this during the breeding season, and also to protect each other while feeding.

Coelophysis is a small carnivore. A flash flood in Mexico revealed the remains of lots of *Coelophysis* that died together.

Meaning of name: Hollow form
Height: 4 ft, 4 in (1.3 m)
Length: 10 ft (3 m)
Family: Coelophysoidea
Period: Late Triassic
Weight: 66 lb (30 kg)
Found in: USA
Diet: Meat

STRENGTH IN NUMBERS?

▼ Sauropod tracks show that the vulnerable young travel with older sauropods of the same species for safety.

▼ Gazelle-like in speed and size, *Hypsilophodon* find greater safety in numbers, as they can keep a better lookout for approaching hunters.

▼ Around 3,500 fossil bones (including 14 skulls) of *Pachyrhinosaurus* have been found in one area of Alberta. They migrate in herds seasonally, in search of food.

CRESTED KILLER

A clunk... a huge weight... and suddenly, you're knocked to the dusty ground. The roaring *Dilophosaurus* seem to be in a panic, and race past at about 25 mph (40 km/h). Fortunately, they don't notice you. What are they running from?

Dilophosaurus' dew claw is an unusual feature. It is similar to the dew claw found on the back of each leg on pet dogs and cats.

Weak jaws mean a weak bite, so this killer probably relies on its sharp claws to bring down its prey.

Dilophosaurus is the largest predator of the early Jurassic period.

Meaning of name: Two-ridged lizard
Height: 5 ft (1.5 m)
Length: 20 ft (6 m)
Family: Coelophysoidea
Period: Early Jurassic
Weight: 1,000 lb (450 kg)
Found in: USA
Diet: Meat

The double crest on the head of *Dilophosaurus* was probably for show, perhaps to make it look taller and more aggressive, and to attract a mate.

HOW MUCH DO WE KNOW?

What do we really know about the appearance of creatures like *Dilophosaurus*?

▶ The crests have never been found attached to the skull, but their position on top of the head is accepted by most scientists as likely to be correct.

▶ Some models of *Dilophosaurus* are covered with hair. Some evidence of hairlike and feather coverings have been found for some prehistoric creatures, such as the birdlike *Archaeopteryx*.

▼ *Dilophosaurus* have been shown with a retractable neck frill, as they were in the movie *Jurassic Park*. There is no evidence of their having had frills, although some reptiles alive today do.

AMBUSH!

You run up over the bank to see the creature the *Dilophosaurus* were terrified of. An *Albertosaurus*—a smaller relative of *Tyrannosaurus rex*—is lumbering along a lakeside. Just as you raise the camera, there's a roar and a splash. A *Deinosuchus* lunges up from the water and grabs its neck. The horror of it makes your head spin.

Another name for *Deinosuchus* is *Phobosuchus*, which means "horror crocodile." With a deadly gigantic 6.5 ft- (2 m-) long head, and an estimated body length of 33 ft (10 m), it's no wonder!

Albertosaurus was probably able to run at 25 mph (40 km/h) in spite of its size. Like *T. rex*, its teeth were not adapted to chewing, so it swallowed meat in large chunks.

Albertosaurus is a powerful killer and was one of the most common predators in Cretaceous North America.

Meaning of name: Alberta lizard
Height: 11 ft (3.4 m)
Length: 30 ft (9 m)
Family: Tyrannosauridae
Period: Late Cretaceous
Weight: 2.8 tons (2,500 kg)
Found in: North America
Diet: Meat

The *Deinosuchus* is a terrifying crocodile that hides in muddy waters, ambushing dinosaurs and snapping up turtles.

KILLING THE KILLERS

In Cretaceous times, hungry creatures lurked in wetland areas, waiting for passing dinosaurs.

► The 100 curved, bone-crunching teeth of the *Deinosuchus* can grasp the throat of a meat-eating dinosaur as it lowers its head to drink.

◄ Cretaceous crocodiles have eyes that can look up out of the water for prey, while their bodies are hidden under the water.

▼ The largest ever crocodile, *Sarcosuchus*, lives in Cretaceous times. Its conical teeth are perfectly shaped for grabbing small dinosaurs and holding them underwater until they drown, ready to be eaten.

ENDGAME

As you set off back to your ATV, the sky suddenly fills with fire. What's happening? A stampede of terrified dinosaurs thunders toward you... and everything goes black. When you come to, you find yourself on a boat heading home, clutching your camera. Perhaps you passed out and the fire-filled sky was all a dream. Or perhaps you just witnessed a new extinction of the dinosaurs.

WHAT KILLED THE DINOSAURS?

After ruling the Earth for 150 million years, the dinosaurs all suddenly died 65 million years ago. There are many theories as to what happened.

◄ A vast asteroid or comet may have collided with the Earth, causing a massive explosion, dust clouds, and shock waves. All around the world, plants and animals would have died.

► Scientists have discovered a vast crater in Mexico that probably formed when an asteroid or comet hit the Earth 65 million years ago. Its 112-mile (180-km) width suggests a catastrophic impact.

▼ In India there were huge volcanic eruptions at the time the dinosaurs died. Vast clouds of ash and dust may have screened out the sun. Plants would have died, then the plant-eaters, and finally the meat-eaters.

KILLER SAFARI REPORT

When you get home, you tell everyone about your safari experience. Crowds gather to hear of your terrifying encounters with killer dinosaurs. When you screen your film, gasps of disbelief fill the auditoriums. The images that get the biggest screams are those of the infamous *Tyrannosaurus rex*!

As you discovered, killers come in all sizes. The small swarming dinosaurs were as deadly as the huge, stumbling monsters. A swipe from the sickle-shaped claw of a 3.3 ft (1 m) *Troodon* could kill you as quickly as a bite from a 16.5 ft (5 m) *Allosaurus*.

T. rex—19 ft, 7 in (6 m)
Allosaurus—16 ft, 5 in (5 m)
Albertosaurus—11 ft (3.4 m)
Carnotaurus—9 ft, 10 in (3 m)
Human—6 ft (1.8 m)

Deinonychus—5 ft (1.5 m)
Dilophosaurus—5 ft (1.5 m)
Troodon—3 ft, 3 in (1 m)
Compsognathus—2 ft, 4 in (0.7 m)

While on your safari, you saw creatures from many different parts of the prehistoric past. This chart shows the different periods in which they lived. MYA stands for million years ago.

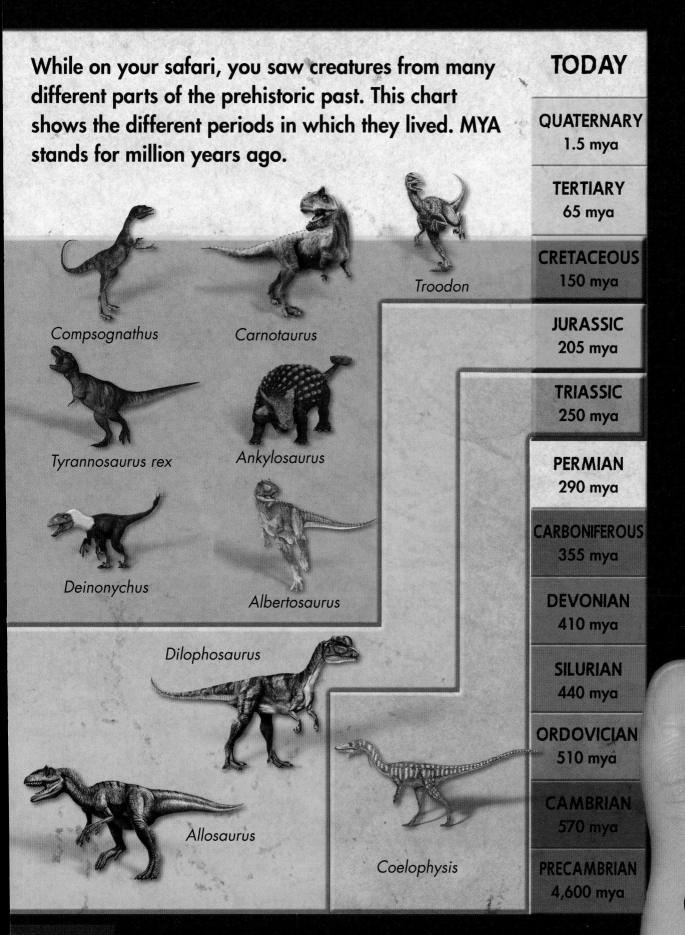

Compsognathus

Carnotaurus

Troodon

Tyrannosaurus rex

Ankylosaurus

Deinonychus

Albertosaurus

Dilophosaurus

Allosaurus

Coelophysis

TODAY	
QUATERNARY	1.5 mya
TERTIARY	65 mya
CRETACEOUS	150 mya
JURASSIC	205 mya
TRIASSIC	250 mya
PERMIAN	290 mya
CARBONIFEROUS	355 mya
DEVONIAN	410 mya
SILURIAN	440 mya
ORDOVICIAN	510 mya
CAMBRIAN	570 mya
PRECAMBRIAN	4,600 mya

GLOSSARY

asteroid A rocky object that orbits the Sun. Asteroids can crash into other planets, such as Earth.

ATV (all terrain vehicle) A three- or four-wheel bike with an engine, soft wheels, and handlebars for off-road travel (also called a quad or quad bike).

binocular vision The way in which the world is seen through two forward-facing eyes, which helps an animal judge distance.

blind A shelter used to hide in while watching wildlife, such as birds.

Brachiosaurus A giant four-legged plant-eater from the Jurassic age.

breeding season Months in the year when animals gather in order to create offspring.

cannibals Animals that eat the flesh of their own kind.

comet An object of ice and dust that travels in space and forms a tail of gas and dust as it passes close to the Sun.

conical Describing a round, pointed shape such as an ice-cream cone.

crampons Spikes that are attached to the bottom of climbers' shoes to grip rock, snow, or ice.

Cretaceous A prehistoric period in which mammals and giant dinosaurs such as *Tyrannosaurus rex* lived, which ended with the mass extinction of the dinosaurs 65 million years ago.

dew claw A claw that does not reach the ground but is positioned higher than the foot, at the back of the leg.

duckbills Dinosaurs with jaws that are shaped like a duck's bill (beak); also called hadrosaurids.

fangs Long, sharp teeth, which are often used for biting and tearing flesh.

fossils Prehistoric remains such as bones, or traces such as footprints, that have become preserved in rock.

horns Pointed bones that stick out from a creature's head, which can be used for attack or defense.

lizard A four-legged reptile with scaly skin and a long tail, such as a chameleon.

mate One of two animals (a male or a female) that have come together to have offspring (babies).

nocturnal vision The ability to see in the dark.

scavenger A creature that feeds on rubbish or dead material, such as the flesh of dead dinosaurs.

serrated With a jagged edge, like the edge of a saw.

shock waves A violent change in air pressure that travels outward from an explosion, causing damage and destruction.

Shunosaurus A four-legged plant-eating dinosaur from the Jurassic age, with a long tail that ends in a spiked club.

sickle A curved shape like the sickle tool, which was used on farms for cutting crops.

skin impressions The shapes made by the surface of the skin: for example the shapes of scales or feathers on a dinosaur, which are preserved as fossils.

stegosaur Four-legged plant-eating dinosaurs, such as *Stegosaurus*, which have two rows of bony plates down their back, a short neck, and small head.

tendons Tough, ropelike tissue in bodies, such as the tissue that attaches muscles to bones.

therapod Two-footed, mainly meat-eating, dinosaurs such as *Tyrannosaurus* and *Giganotosaurus*.

FURTHER READING

Dinosaur Encyclopedia by Caroline Bingham (Dorling Kindersley, 2009)

Dinosaur Experience by John Malam (Dorling Kindersley, 2006)

Dinosaurus: The Complete Guide to Dinosaurs by Steve Parker (Firefly, 2009)

Tyrannosaurus Rex Vs Velociraptor: Power Against Speed (Dinosaur Wars) by Michael O'Hearn (Raintree, 2011)

The Mystery of the Death of the Dinosaurs (Can Science Solve?) by Chris Oxlade (Heinemann Library, 2008)

Predators (Dinosaur Files) by John Malam (Dorling Kindersley, 2009)

WEB SITES

www.kidsdinos.com/ Dinosaurs for Kids—fun facts, games and a dinosaur database

www.nhm.ac.uk/kids-only/dinosaurs/index. html London's Natural History Museum—includes a dinosaur directory and quiz

www.amnh.org/exhibitions/fightingdinos/—information about the American Museum of Natural History's "Fighting Dinosaurs"

http://dsc.discovery.com Discovery Dinosaur Central—search the DinoViewer for size comparisons and how dinosaurs moved

http://ngm.nationalgeographic.com National Geographic—search for the Bizarre Dinosaur section for a closer look at strange dinosaurs

http://www.enchantedlearning.com/ subjects/dinosaurs/ Zoom Dinosaurs—basic to advanced information on dinosaurs and prehistory

INDEX